The Queen –

A Sacred Rebellion of Remembering

A Manifesto for the Invisible, the Awakened and the Becoming

By

R. Allure

It is time... You have been invited...

The Queen.

Where The Prince teaches power through fear,

The Queen remembers that fear is a wound.

She rules through wholeness.

She does not divide and conquer.

She unites and transforms.

Her realm begins within.

Introduction

There comes a moment — sometimes loud, sometimes whisper-soft — when the life you have been living no longer fits. The shape of you has shifted, and the shell that once held you is now too tight, too dull, too small. You begin to feel the friction: in your body, in your thoughts, in the aching silence between what you were taught to want and what your soul actually yearns for.

This is not a breakdown.

It is a breaking open.

A remembering.

I am **The Queen**, not by bloodline or inheritance, but by reclamation. I speak not for a monarchy, but for a multitude. The women. The forgotten. The becoming. The ones who have been labelled too much or not enough — and who are now choosing to step forward, sovereign in silence, radiant in purpose.

This book is not a manual.

It is a mirror.

It is a spell.

It is a map, written five times over — as is our way — by every woman who chooses to awaken and write herself back into the sacred story.

Welcome to the reclamation.

Welcome to the invisibility game. Where power is a paradox because it is found in invisibility - the space between

Welcome home.

Chapter 1

The Invisibility Game

And the Power We Never Lost

They told us invisibility was weakness.

But they were wrong.

Invisibility — when chosen — is not disappearance.

It is precision.

It is power.

It is presence beyond performance.

When we stop being seen in the way the world demands — filtered, palatable, pleasing — we begin to see ourselves. Truly. Undistorted. Unclaimed. And in that seeing, a portal opens.

The Invisibility Game is not about hiding.

It is about reclaiming the unseen self.

The self not reduced to appearance, productivity or performance.

The self who listens deeply, moves wisely, and acts only when alignment calls.

And when the world no longer hears your footsteps, you can go anywhere.

We did not lose our power.

We gave it away.

Now we take it back — not by force, but by focus and reconnection

And when we become invisible by choice, we become untouchable by design.

An insight from The Queen when she suddenly understood invisibility was power:

They mistook our invisibility for absence.

But we were never gone.

We were watching, learning, remembering.

There is a profound joy in becoming invisible — not to hide, but to unbind.

When you are no longer the object of the world's projections, you are free to become the subject of your own becoming.

Invisibility is not erasure. It is liberation from the constant distortion of the gaze — from being boxed, explained, dismissed, reduced.

It is the art of stepping back, not out.

It is where we stop performing and begin being.

To be invisible is to choose what is seen.

To move between the seen and unseen with wisdom, to preserve your energy for what matters,

and to withdraw your magic from systems that only want to drain it.

Invisibility allows us to reclaim time, intuition and presence.

To hear our own voice without interruption.

To gather, to nourish, to prepare.

To weave our webs without the world watching, criticising, or co-opting.

This is why invisibility is a game.

Not because it is trivial — but because it requires play, skill and strategy.

It is a reclamation of agency, a return to the sacred art of feminine movement: fluid, unpredictable, powerful.

The game is not to vanish — it is to choose when to appear.

To disrupt with elegance.

To protect with precision.

To build without needing permission.

You see, the game is not about hiding.

It is about revealing deliberately.

And when the moment comes — we do not scream.

We ripple.

We do not march in lines.

We swarm.

This is not weakness.

It is a different kind of strength.

The kind that does not need to prove itself.

The kind that smiles, knowing the world will one day wonder:

"Where did they go?"

And then, "How did they do this?"

We are not lost.

We are not broken.

We are not silent.

We are invisible by choice.

And oh, what joy there is in that.

— The Queen

Chapter 2

Perspective and Opportunity

"If the girls are broken, so is the world — and therein lies our sacred opportunity."

The Queen does not avert her gaze from pain — she leans in. She listens to the aching silence beneath the noise. To the inner collapse inside women who feel too much, love too deep and bend too far to be accepted.

She looks out at culture — not with hatred, but with truth-clarity.

This world is not just unjust — it is out of rhythm with soul.

It trains us to conform, consume, compare — not to create, connect or commune.

It shapes girls to be pleasing before powerful.

It denies boys softness and exiles their tears.

"This world was not built for wholeness.

But we — we remember how to rebuild."

From the Queen's perspective, what society calls failure is often the threshold of becoming. What it calls madness may be spiritual emergence. And what it labels brokenness might be the body's cry for truth.

She sees clearly: the culture that breaks the girls also betrays the boys — and thereby betrays itself.

We are not just healing individuals.

We are realigning civilization.

"If the girls are broken, so is the world — and therein lies our sacred opportunity."

This is not a call to burn it all down.

This is a call to build from truth.

To shape structures from soul.

To design from dignity.

The Queen reminds us:

You can rage and still be radiant.

You can grieve and still be grounded.

You can see the destruction and still create beauty.

The masculine is not the enemy — unconsciousness is.

We do not need more domination or erasure.

We need reverent power.

Aligned polarity.

The divine interplay of inner worlds, in sacred motion.

"The old world teaches us to be afraid of our power.

The new world asks us to wield it —
wisely."

This is the perspective of the Queen —

To see where the world is cracking and offer seeds.

To see where culture is lost, and bring rhythm.

To see where the girls are hurting, and build the new temple there.

Because brokenness is not the end.

It is the beginning of remembering.

And in remembering — we rise.

The world may call our girls broken. We say they are beginning.

To see a crack as a fault is the old way. To see it as the place where light enters is the truth. For every woman who has been called too loud, too sensitive, too soft, too fierce — we see you. You are exactly as you were meant to be.

Culture taught us to numb. To shrink. To disappear by becoming palatable. But we remember now:

The system is not broken. It is functioning exactly as designed.

But we were never made for that system.

This is our opportunity.

To choose not to fix ourselves but to free ourselves.

To design not a better cage, but a wider sky.

The Queen does not demand a world that fits her.

She builds a world that reflects her.

And invites others to do the same.

There is a new perspective through the eyes of the Queen, through the fractures of culture, through the womb of what is possible.

Chapter 3

Grace, Reaction & Response

There is a space between stimulus and action — a sacred pause. That is where the Queen lives.

In a world addicted to immediacy and reactivity, she chooses her rhythm. She chooses grace.

Reaction is survival.

Response is sovereignty.

Reaction is the echo of old pain. It is the wound speaking before the soul has a chance to breathe. But response... response is born from awareness. From stillness. From presence.

Grace is not weakness. It is restraint with wisdom. It is fire with discernment. It is the ability to see the game being played and choose not to play by old rules.

The Queen has no need to prove, to defend or to win small battles. She is playing a longer game.

She knows her peace is her power.

And so she breathes.

She waits.

She listens.

She responds — when she is ready, in a way that aligns with her truth.

And sometimes, her silence is the loudest response of all.

There are times she has descended and she accepts that because she is human:

The Queen's Fall and Return

The Queen did not fall physically.

She was pushed — by the weight of every voice that told her she could not hold her own light.

And still, she did not give in. Yes it hurt but against all odds she rose.

Not because she believed in herself. But because she chose to try anyway.

Self-doubt did not disappear.

It walked beside her.

But she did not feed it.

It was part of the journey.

A strengthening process.

A process of preparation for what was to come.

She had a choice and…

She continued…

The queen wrote through it.

She danced with doubt.

She loved herself louder than the voice that told her not to.

Excerpt from The Queen's own writing: On Opinion and the Self

"You will never be free if you live inside another's opinion."

"Criticism is often the echo of someone else's unhealed wound."

"You do not owe the world likability. You owe it integrity."

"Love yourself loudly. It is an act of rebellion."

… Chapter 4

Boundaries, Respect & Raising the Future

We teach not with our words, but with our lives.

How we allow ourselves to be treated becomes the blueprint for how the next generation believes love should feel. We speak of kindness, but do we show our daughters how to say no without apology? Do we show our sons how to honour a boundary without being bruised by it?

Boundaries are not barriers.

They are bridges to self-respect.

To say "this is where I end, and you begin" is not separation — it is clarity.

Respect must be taught in how we listen. How we pause. How we honour both our softness and our strength.

If a girl is taught she must be agreeable to be accepted, she learns to abandon herself for belonging.

If a boy is taught that dominance is his birth-right, he may never learn how to truly connect.

So we rewrite the scripts.

We raise children not for a broken system, but for a sacred future.

One where boys are not shamed for gentleness and girls are not punished for power.

Where love is not possession, but presence.

Where respect is not earned but offered and given through appreciation.

The Queen raises the future not with fear, but with fierce tenderness.

Chapter 5

Wealth, Money & Receiving

The Queen's Reclamation of Sacred Abundance

They told us that wealth must be earned through exhaustion.

That money was power and power was to be feared or fought.

That to receive without suffering was selfish.

They were wrong.

Wealth is not your worth.

It is the by-product of your contribution.

The natural response of a world that benefits when you are fully expressed.

The Queen does not chase wealth.

She becomes it.

She understands that the most powerful currency in the world is alignment, her health and her radiance.

"To receive is not weakness.

It is wisdom."

"You are not here to sacrifice your joy for survival.

 You are here to create so richly, the world cannot help but respond."

She no longer worships the old gods of scarcity and self-denial.

She gives her devotion to creativity, generosity, and circulation.

She knows:

Wealth is not accumulation. It is activation.

Money is not shameful. It is neutral. It takes the shape of its holder.

Receiving is not greedy. It is gracious. It fuels the mission.

The Queen waters her work with abundance.

She plants ideas in the rich soil of inspiration.

She creates not to compete — but to contribute.

"You do not need to burn out to prove your value. You are already the proof."

And when she receives, she receives fully.

With open palms.

With softened heart.

With zero guilt and deep gratitude.

She knows the flow of abundance isn't one-directional.

It is circular.

And her part is to give from overflow — not depletion.

She surrounds herself with beauty — not as vanity, but as vibration.

She honours the wealth within — the ideas, the wisdom, the presence.

She builds her queendom not on scarcity, but on sacred circulation.

This is not about manifesting a mansion.

This is about embodying the frequency of enoughness.

Where money becomes a river — not a ruler.

Where you no longer shrink to survive — But rise to resonate.

You are your wealth.

Your voice. Your gifts. Your inner garden.

When you live in full bloom — the world blooms with you.

Chapter 6

Sacred Emotion & Inner Alchemy

There is no such thing as a bad emotion. Only an unprocessed one.

The Queen does not suppress her anger. She sculpts with it.

She does not deny her fear. She listens. She learns. She lets it teach her where her edges are.

She is not ruled by her emotions — she is refined by them.

Love and hate, anger and fear — these are not opposites. They are twin flames, dancing in the fire of transformation. Every emotion is a messenger. Every sensation is sacred.

The body does not lie.

Emotions are information.

Stored too long, they become inflammation.

Ignored too long, they become illness.

We are not meant to internalise pain.

We are meant to move it to meet it, to let it move through.

The Queen breathes into discomfort, alchemising rage into boundaries, sorrow into beauty, love into fuel. She lets each emotion pass through the temple of her body like a prayer.

And in doing so, she becomes the most dangerous force of all:

A woman in alignment with her own truth, her own body, her own wisdom.

The Myth of the Three Selves

They say a woman carries three Selves:

The Shadow, who learned to survive.

The Flame, who dares to transform.

The Crown, who remembers who she is.

The Shadow built masks and rejected the parts that did not please or conform.

The Flame burns the masks and reignites the parts denied before integrating and accepting them.

And the Crown… she walks barefaced into her life embodying the whole of her being.

But you cannot wear the Crown without first thanking the Shadow for all she did to protect you and keep you alive.

Chapter 7

Love, Relationships & The Inner Worlds

We were never taught how to love ourselves. We were taught how to perform worthiness.

And so we sought love in places that could never hold us. We confused intensity with intimacy, attention with affection and sacrifice with devotion.

But the Queen... she remembers.

Real love begins inside.

And the inner world creates the outer relationship.

She no longer seeks someone to complete her — for she is not broken. She does not need to be rescued — for she is not lost. She invites connection not from emptiness, but from overflow.

When the masculine and feminine energies come into alignment — within and without — love becomes ignition, not dependency.

The sacred masculine does not shrink before her power — he rises.

The divine feminine does not dim for his light — she shines in resonance.

True partnership is not two halves joining.

It is two wholes walking in alignment - in symbiosis.

She knows her energy — its pulse, its truth, its magnetism. And so, she senses the resonance. She knows when love is rooted in recognition, not projection.

She doesn't chase. She doesn't fix.

She attracts by being, not by bending.

And when she chooses to open her heart, she does so not in desperation, but in devotion. Not in fear, but in fierce clarity. She knows.

For love, in its highest form, is not about possession or performance — it is about presence.

It is not what someone gives you. It is what awakens in you when truth is near.

Chapter 8

Radiance & Reverence

They sold us youth as beauty.

But it was never youth that made us beautiful.

It was aliveness. It was presence. It was truth.

They taught us to resist time, erase lines, numb softness.

To freeze the stories in our faces.

To chase a standard that was never ours.

But the Queen does not modify herself to be accepted.

She magnifies herself to radiate and ignite.

She wears her lines like lightning bolts of wisdom.

She walks with the weight of experience like a crown.

And when she laughs — the whole sky listens.

She does not carve herself into society's mold.

She softens into her own sacred shape.

The scars? She honours them.

The flabby bits? She loves them, too.

The unevenness, the stretch, the curve — all the living proof that she has been here.

"The imperfections are not flaws. They are invitations."

"Wisdom lives in the lines. The love sparkles through the eyes."

"The universe does not whisper through the edited — it roars through the embodied."

This is not decay.

This is deepening.

This is the sacred privilege of continuing.

Let them chase the illusion.

We choose embodiment.

We choose the velvet of self-knowing over the varnish of perfection.

We choose reverence for the vessel that has carried us through fire and still sings.

Aging is not a loss of beauty.
It is the revealing of it.

You are not fading.
You are ripening.

Chapter 9

When We Ignore the Alarms

At first, the soul whispers. Then it knocks. Then it roars.

We are not punished by ignoring our intuition — we are redirected. Nudged. Shaken. Silenced. Until finally, we can no longer ignore the discomfort.

But in a world addicted to numbing — we learn to silence the alarms.

We stay too long. In relationships. In jobs. In roles. In identities we've outgrown.

We tolerate noise, chaos, disconnection — and call it normal.

Until one day the body speaks louder than the brain.

And the Queen realises: the alarms were never the enemy.

They were the invitation.

Anxiety is often intuition that's been ignored.

Burnout is the soul's way of saying: enough.

Numbness is not peace — it is the cost of not listening.

The Queen knows this now.

And so she chooses differently.

She listens the first time.

She honours the tingle in her belly, the tightness in her chest, the flutter in her knowing.

She hears the whispers — and acts before the roar.

Because her life is no longer built on survival.

It is sculpted by listening.

And when the alarms no longer need to scream, the soul can finally sing.

Chapter 10

When We Stop Hearing the Alarms

There was a time I silenced the alarms. Not out of ignorance, but out of survival.

You see, my love, the alarms are not always loud.

They begin as whispers.

A clench in the gut.

A twitch behind the eyes.

A sigh you didn't even realise escaped your lips.

They are sacred signals — the body's tender way of saying, "Something is not right here."

But the world taught you not to listen. It told you to smile when your soul wept.

To stay when your spirit begged you to run. To please. To push. To pretend.

And so, over time, you taught your heart to quieten.

You labelled the discomfort "drama."

You called the rage "too much."

You wore the numbness like armour and called it coping.

But let me tell you, dear one: When you stop hearing the alarms, you begin to betray yourself in the most subtle of ways.

Not all at once. Not in a grand collapse. But drip by sacred drip.

The slow erosion of aliveness.

And then one day, you realise you don't feel much at all.

Not the joy. Not the ache. Just a kind of quiet exhaustion that lives in your bones.

You wonder how you got here.

And I say: The alarms were sounding. You were just too conditioned to listen.

But don't be ashamed. This forgetting is common. It is part of the fracture we are taught to carry.

You were not meant to override your instincts. You were meant to live in rhythm with them.

Let me share a truth:

Strength is not in the silencing.

Power is not in the ignoring.

Grace is not in the endurance of what harms you.

True power is remembering.

Honouring the body's knowing.

Honouring the whispers before they become screams.

And when the screams do come — meeting them with reverence.

Because every alarm you ever silenced was a gift.

An invitation back home.

And when you begin to hear again — really hear — you'll find that the body never stopped loving you. It was simply waiting for your return.

I do not call this weakness.

I call this reunion.

I call this Queenship.

So now, I ask you gently:

Where have you silenced yourself?

Where have you labelled truth as inconvenience?

And where are the alarms still sounding — quietly, patiently — waiting for you to listen?

Come back to yourself.

Not with judgement.

With curiosity. With compassion. With courage.

Because when you honour the alarms,

you restore your sovereignty.

And that…

That is the beginning of your return.

To you. To truth. To the Queen within.

Chapter 11

Avoidance, Attitude & Responsibility

The Queen knows this truth: avoidance is a thief.

It steals time, integrity, clarity and power.

Avoidance wears many masks — procrastination, overthinking, people-pleasing, false positivity. But underneath it all is fear. Fear of failure. Fear of truth. Fear of being fully seen.

But the Queen chooses a different path.

She understands that attitude is not just perspective — it's energetic leadership.

Her attitude determines her altitude. And so she takes responsibility not as a burden, but as a birth-right.

Responsibility is not blame. It is agency.

It is the art of saying, "This is mine to carry and this is not."

There is a difference between endurance and enjoyment.

Between suffering for the sake of survival and choosing a life that nourishes.

The Queen is done with enduring.

She is here to embody. To enjoy. To expand.

And she knows that true joy is not a result of perfect circumstances — but of honest alignment.

She transforms "I have to" into "I choose to."

She moves from reaction into reclamation.

She no longer abandons herself to keep the peace.

Because peace is not the absence of conflict.

Peace is the presence of truth.

"On Service."

"Service is not submission. It is not the shaming of the self for the comfort of others.

True service is sacred contribution — the art of giving yourself to what is worthy.

If you cannot love people, then serve the land.

If you do not trust the world, then tend the roots beneath it.

Gaia receives what we forget.

She too has been raped, ridiculed, burned, violated, silenced, and sold.

And she, too, is remembering herself."

"When you remember who you are, your hands ache to create something of worth.

Not for applause. Not for status. But because the soul cannot stay silent when the world begins to break."

Chapter 12

Gaia — The Remembering of Earth

She is not a resource. She is a relative.

Before there were systems, borders, or beliefs, there was Her.

The Earth. Gaia. The first mother. The original altar.

And she does not belong to us.

We belong to her.

We were never meant to conquer her.

We were meant to commune with her.

To live in devotion, not domination.

To remember that soil is not separate from soul.

 "You are not here to conquer Earth. You are here to remember her."

"If destruction is manmade, then devotion must be woman-willed."

Gaia does not punish.

She responds.

She echoes back what we have forgotten — that every extraction has a consequence and every act of reverence becomes a seed.

She is not fragile — she is ferocious.

And she is remembering.

She remembers how to burn.

How to flood.

How to cleanse what has forgotten its source.

And still — she loves us.

She absorbs our toxins.

She swallows our violence.

She waits for our return.

We must become the women who return to the Earth, not just as visitors, but as keepers of the sacred, stewards of balance, guardians of beauty.

This is not environmentalism.

This is reverence.

This is not charity.

This is kinship.

This is not optional.

This is our sacred commitment.

The Queen remembers:

That the Earth is not just the ground beneath us — she is the body of us.

That to love Gaia is to love life.

That to listen to the Earth is to hear the soul of the world.

We plant, not just to grow food, but to grow futures.

We tend, not just to harvest, but to heal.

We walk gently, not in fear, but in fierce loyalty to what holds us all.

This is how the world changes:

From the ground up.

From remembering down to the roots.

From the sacred soil of our collective becoming.

Chapter 13

Destruction & Devotion

Excerpt from The Queen: Destruction & Devotion

There are always two paths to power.
One paved in extraction.
The other rooted in **reciprocity**.

One climbs by conquest, always hungry, always hollow. The other rises by relationship — whole, rooted, awake.

The Queen has walked both.
She has tasted the sharpness of self-abandonment.
She has seen what happens when power is severed from care.
And she has turned back. Chosen again.
Planted differently.

"There are two paths to power: extraction or reciprocity.
One leaves you hollow. The other, whole."

We were not sent here to conquer the Earth.
We are of her. We are her memory, her midwives, her mirror.

"You are not here to conquer Earth. You are here to remember her."

And just as destruction is manmade, Devotion must now be **woman-willed**.

Not soft. Not passive. Not poetic for its own sake.
But **active devotion** — fierce, intelligent, embodied love.
Love that builds ecosystems.
Love that rewires economies.
Love that refuses to play by rules rooted in lack and domination.

This is not about blaming man.
It is about balancing forces.
It is about choosing creation where we once chose collapse.

"If destruction is manmade, then devotion must be woman-willed."

The Queen creates from wholeness.
She devotes herself — not as sacrifice, but as **sovereignty**.
Because when a woman stands in sacred reciprocity with life,
She cannot be owned, sold or silenced.

She is power.
And she is enough.

Chapter 14

And the Body...

Excerpt from The Queen: Loving the Body as a Homeland

The Queen does not love her body like a possession.

She loves it like a homeland.

Not as something to be improved, trimmed, covered or praised by external eyes —

But as sacred ground.

The place where her spirit touches Earth.

She does not extract from it, she plants within it.

She does not conquer it with discipline, she listens with reverence.

She rests here. She rises here. She returns home here.

Her body is not an accessory to achievement.

It is her instrument of alignment — the first place she learns truth, the first field she protects, the first temple she tends.

"She defends it with sacred rage when needed.

And praises it not for what it looks like — but for how it lets her resonate with life."

The Queen does not rise to power through perfection.

She returns to it through presence.

Through nourishment, not conquest.

Through resonance, not force.

She speaks fluently in the language of sensation — The ache, the flutter, the pulse beneath silence.

She learns to trust her hungers.

Not just for food, but for touch, stillness, movement, voice, creation.

Pain is no longer her punishment. It becomes her prophecy.

A messenger. A compass. A call to become.

"She transforms her pain into prophecy. And her presence into power."

In a world that taught her to dissociate, she re-inhabits.

In a system that taught her to shrink, she expands.

Where shame was planted, she grows sovereignty.

Because a Queen who lives in her body — fully, fiercely, joyfully — Is a revolution the world cannot unsense.

Chapter 15

Truth & Sovereignty

Truth is not always comfortable.

But it is always liberating.

The Queen has stopped outsourcing her knowing.

She no longer waits for permission to feel what she feels, to know what she knows or to speak what must be said.

She is sovereign — not because she rules over others, but because she refuses to be ruled by fear, guilt or inherited belief.

Sovereignty is self-leadership in its purest form.

It is the ability to listen, discern and choose — from within.

No longer does she bend herself into socially acceptable shapes. No longer does she wear masks to keep others safe from her magnitude. Her truth is not always easy — but it is hers. And that makes it sacred.

She holds her truth like a flame. Sometimes it flickers. Sometimes it roars. But it always guides.

And in her sovereignty, she remembers:

She does not need to be understood by all.

She only needs to be in alignment with herself.

That is itself is liberation.

Chapter 16

Legacy & Leadership

From the Throne Within

Leadership is not a title.

It is a transmission.

A frequency you carry in your spine, not on your business card.

Legacy is not what you leave behind when you're gone.

It's what you activate while you're here.

It's not carved into buildings — it's etched into nervous systems, remembered in the lives you've touched, the truths you've dared to live.

The Queen does not lead from dominance.

She leads from depth.

She does not demand allegiance.

She inspires remembrance.

She does not chase visibility.

She stands in energetic clarity and the world rearranges to meet her.

She does not command the room.

She becomes the room. Her presence ignites the room peacefully.

In this new world, leadership is not about who speaks the loudest.

It is about who listens the deepest. Not about control, but coherence.

Not about being followed, but about sparking sovereignty in others.

The Queen builds legacies of integrity — not empire.

She walks first so others know they can.

She becomes the proof, the evidence of possibility.

"Leadership is no longer about telling others where to go or what to do. It is about remembering who you are — so they remember too."

Legacy, in this sacred rebellion, is embodied change.

It is the ripple of a woman who no longer abandons herself.

It is the resonance of a truth so alive, it outlives her breath.

And this is the new leadership:

Devotion without martyrdom.

Power without performance.

Impact without ego.

Truth without apology.

This is how we lead now.

As Queens.

As Builders.

As Mirrors.

As Midwives of the world to come.

Chapter 17

Self Love — A Fierce Reverence

They sold us self-love like a product.

Pretty. Packaged. Palatable.

"Take a day off."

"Light a candle."

"Buy the cream."

"Say the mantra."

But the Queen remembers what the world forgot:

"This is self-love:

Not bubble baths or hashtags... But a fierce loyalty to your aliveness and your existence."

It is not always soft.

It is often a roaring no.

A sacred boundary.

A refusal to shrink.

A decision to rest — not as escape, but as devotion.

Self-love is the moment she stops betraying herself to belong.

It is when she speaks, even if her voice shakes.

It is the courage to walk away from what erodes her soul — no matter how gilded the offering.

It is kissing her own wounds.

Naming her own worth.

And staying with herself, especially in the silence.

"And when you treat yourself with reverence, the world begins to respond in kind — or it falls away."

That fall is a blessing. What cannot meet her in love, in truth, in wholeness — was never hers to carry.

She does not need the world to approve of her glow.

She only needs to stand in it.

Because when a woman truly loves herself — not for how she looks, but for how she lives — she becomes unshakeable.

And that is the kind of beauty the world cannot buy, tame, or deny.

Chapter 18

Fight, Flight, Feminine

"They trained you to run or destroy."

"But you forgot the third response: the Feminine."

"Not weak. Not frozen. But wide awake presence."

"We do not fight their wars. We reprogram their fields."

"We do not flee the world. We reseed it."

For centuries, the world offered us two doors:

Fight — and become like them.

Flight — escape as quickly as possible.

And so many of us, confused by the violence of it all, either burned ourselves out in battle or made ourselves small enough to vanish.

But the Queen remembers the third door. The Feminine.

The feminine is not passive — it is precise.

It is not aggressive — it is alchemical.

It does not flee from chaos — it composts it into clarity.

When the fight calls, we don't rage — we recalibrate.

When the urge to flee arises, we don't vanish — we root.

We enter the field of distortion not to react, but to restructure it with frequency, focus, and unwavering presence.

This is not spiritual bypass. This is spiritual combat — conducted with grace, not grenades. With vision, not vengeance.

"They taught us to wield weapons or wounds. We remembered how to wield energy."

In a world obsessed with dominance, the feminine becomes the quiet revolution.

In a system designed for control, she becomes the code breaker.

She need not raise her voice.

She need only remember her power.

Because when she stands fully in herself, the system cannot contain her.

And the world begins to change — not by force, but by field.

Chapter 19

Cycles & Rebirth

The Queen does not fear endings.

She understands that death is a doorway.

Seasons fall away. Versions of her dissolve. Old names, roles, and identities burn in sacred fire. Not because she is lost — but because she is returning.

Rebirth is not about becoming someone else. It is about remembering who you were before the forgetting.

She lives cyclically — like the moon, the womb, the earth. She understands that growth is not linear. It spirals. It deepens. It repeats what needs healing until it is seen with love.

Every contraction is followed by expansion. Every descent brings hidden treasure.

She does not rush the winter or chase the spring.

She honours them all — because she knows she is all of it.

Death. Birth. Becoming. Again. Again. Again.

Excerpt from The Queen's own reflections: The Rhythm of Becoming

"Before there was language, there was rhythm."

"Before there was hierarchy, there was pulse."

"To know your future, move your body until it speaks."

"She who remembers her rhythm cannot be controlled."

"She will not burn the world. She will regrow it."

Chapter 20

On Boxes, Cages & Other Lies We Were Told

They offered us boxes: neat, labelled, sealed. And we — in our innocence — stepped in.

Be a good girl. Be nice. Be pretty. Be quiet. Be small.

Fit in. Please. Perfect. Perform.

But the Queen outgrew the box.

The silk lining wore thin. The air got tight. The truth got loud.

A cage wrapped in comfort is still a cage.

A golden rulebook is still a leash.

We were never meant to fit inside someone else's story.

We were meant to write our own.

And so, she unlearned the lie that safety comes from sameness. That belonging means bending. That love must be earned through obedience.

She shattered the cage.

Stepped into the wild.

And in that breaking, found her wings.

The Queen reflecting On Boxes and Cages

"They will build you a rut and call it a career.

They will lace your silence and conformity with silk and call it feminine."

"They will reward your compromise, until you forget the cost of it."

"Fitting in is not safety — it's amnesia."

"Do not fear being unrecognisable to the old world. Fear being a stranger to your own soul."

Excerpt from The Queen: On Self-Worth and Reclamation

"You were not born to be pleasing.

You were born to be powerful."

"Reclaiming yourself will feel like rebellion.

Because they purposely trained you to doubt your own compass."

"There is nothing radical about wanting liberty.

But there is something revolutionary about taking it."

"Take it gently. Take it fiercely. But take it."

Chapter 21

The Law of Mirrors

"There will come a day when what you have done unto us will be done unto you."

"Not in violence. Not in vengeance. But in energetic law."

"To awaken the soul, the ego must taste its own creation."

Energy does not lie.

Frequency does not forget.

And the Universe — in all her fierce intelligence — does not punish, but she reflects.

What is done in distortion must, eventually, be seen in full clarity.

Not so we suffer.

But so we awaken.

Every suppression returns to sender.

Every silencing echoes louder.

Every projection circles back — not to shame, but to show what must be healed.

This is not revenge.

This is restoration.

"The Law of Mirrors does not seek retribution. It seeks recognition."

Until a soul has felt the wound it inflicts, it will never understand the healing it must offer.

And so… the mirrors come.

In faces we judged.

In systems we upheld.

In wounds we tried to ignore.

The Queen does not rage at the mirror.

She studies it.

She feels it.

She transcends it.

Because only by facing the mirror can we truly remember:

We were never powerless — only misdirected.

We were never broken — only fragmented.

And as each soul meets its own reflection, a reckoning unfolds. Not to destroy the world — but to remake it.

With clarity.

With compassion.

With consciousness.

Chapter 22

Core Values — The Queen's Compass

"They taught you to earn your worth. Through good grades. Soft smiles. Being liked. Being useful. But the Queen is not liked. She is sovereign.

She does not barter her truth for approval."

"Your value was never in question. It was only hidden beneath conditioning."

"Self-respect is not arrogance. It is the decision to have your own back in a world that feeds on your insecurity."

"The Queen does not seek to impress. She seeks to express. Not for others — but because she must."

The world tries to sell you values: success, popularity, compliance, perfection.

But the Queen...

She digs deep. She asks:

What do I stand for when no one is watching?

What would I protect, even if it costs me comfort?

Her core values are not performative. They are cellular.

They are not taught — they are remembered.

Integrity. Courage. Compassion. Clarity.

Devotion. Liberation. Truth. Wholeness.

These are not ideals.

They are her compass.

She does not trade her values for validation.

She does not silence her soul to keep the peace.

And in holding her values sacred, she holds herself sacred, too.

Because a Queen with values cannot be bought.

And a woman who knows her truth cannot be moved.

Chapter 23

The Queen: On Silence and Solitude

"Solitude is not absence. It is return."

"There is a sound beneath the noise. You can only hear it when you stop speaking."

"What they feared most was that you would go quiet long enough to hear your own truth rise."

Emotional Alchemy: The Queen's Inner Laboratory

The Queen knows that emotions are not enemies — they are messengers, chemicals, and teachers in motion.

She does not suppress what rises within her — she studies it, feels it fully, then transmutes it into power. Because emotion, when internalised without awareness becomes corrosion.

It etches itself into the soft tissue of the body — into organs, breath, bone, and blood.

Hate, when denied or projected, burns blindly. But when seen, it becomes discernment sharpened by boundaries.

Fear, unspoken, calcifies. It crouches in the nervous system, reshaping posture, breath and trust.

But when faced, it becomes a guardian of sacred caution — a compass pointing toward growth.

Anger, left to rot in silence, becomes self-harm. It eats at the liver, the voice, the skin.

But when honoured and moved wisely, it becomes clarity in motion — the fire that initiates transformation.

Love, when authentic, is not weak. It is biological coherence — it harmonises heart and brain rhythms, boosts immunity, restores cells and expands perception. It is the highest healer, the deepest resonance and the original language of the Queen.

The Queen does not abandon emotion.

She welcomes it into the inner chamber.

She listens, moves it and learns from it.

She knows the body keeps a tally but also holds the tools to rewrite the script.

She bathes her nervous system in grace.

She breathes into her cellular memory.

She speaks forgiveness not just as poetry but as biochemical liberation.

Every emotion becomes a frequency of cultivation.

She composts the rage.

She distils the grief.

She reframes the fear.

She softens the hate.

And she chooses — again and again — to return to Love.

This is not avoidance.

It is alchemy.

It is regency over reaction.

It is the Queen, ruling from the inside out.

Chapter 24

Sacred Union: The Queen on Love, Energy & Inner Worlds

The Queen does not chase love. She embodies it.

She understands that relationship is not about possession, obligation or conformity — but resonance.

She is not seeking to be completed. She is seeking to be met — soul to soul, energy to energy, in the honest light of presence.

She has met herself in her depths — the raw, unguarded, radiant, wounded and rising self.

And because she knows her own terrain, she can sense when another carries the resonance of truth.

The Queen understands that love is an energetic equation.

It is not about gender — it is about polarity, integration and alignment.

When the feminine energy within her flows freely — it is receptive, intuitive, creative, magnetic.

It is the river.

When the masculine energy within her is steady — it is grounded, directional, present and holding.

It is the banks of the river.

In sacred partnership — inner or outer — these energies must dance, not dominate.

When two beings come together with their own inner masculine and feminine in balance — what emerges is not dependency, but synergy. They ignite, rather than consume.

They reflect, rather than project.

She has learned that the wrong energy feels like distortion — a pull that drains, a connection that controls, a love that requires effort or for her to shrink or silence her sovereignty.

The right energy is not always easy — but it is clean.

It resonates through the chest, through the breath, through the silence between words.

It feels like coming home to something she didn't know she remembered.

The Queen teaches that before seeking union with another, we must become sovereign within.

You must know your shadows so they do not sabotage your longing.

You must tend to your wounds so you do not bleed on your beloved.

You must know how to hold yourself so you do not demand others hold your wholeness.

Love begins in the inner world.

In the conversations you have with yourself.

In the way you soothe your fears, honour your needs and speak to your reflection.

From this space, you no longer need love to fill a void — you are overflowing with it.

You are not seeking a saviour.

You are calling in a mirror, a witness, a wild dance partner who is also committed to their inner fire.

In alignment, the masculine does not suppress the feminine — he amplifies her magic, grounds her vision, holds her storms and worships her becoming.

And the feminine does not shrink in the presence of the masculine — she awakens him, draws out his depth, ignites his clarity and softens his charge.

Together, they do not complete one another. They amplify the sacred in each other.

This is not a fairy-tale. It is a frequency.
And once felt — it cannot be unfelt.

Chapter 25

The Queen on Attitude, Avoidance & Sacred Responsibility

The Queen has come to understand: attitude is alchemy.

It is not just how we think — it is how we carry ourselves in the face of what is.

She has faced storms that could have broken her — but instead, she asked:

"What part of me is being called to rise?"

This is the power of responsibility.

Not blame. Not burden.

But the radical act of responding with clarity, grace and presence.

To take responsibility is to step into authorship.

It is to no longer outsource your experience to circumstance, luck, or lineage.

It is to say, "I cannot always choose what happens — but I can choose how I show up for it."

But the Queen also knows the lure of avoidance.

It wears many masks:

Perfectionism.

Distraction.

Blame.

The endless scroll. The constant busyness.

Avoidance is the child of fear — and fear, when unacknowledged, breeds disconnection.

Disconnection from self. From intuition. From truth.

But when she finally turns to face what she avoids, it does not grow more powerful — she does.

She once believed life was meant to be endured —

that effort equalled worth,

that struggle proved value,

that to grind was to earn love.

But the Queen unlearned this lie.

Endurance has its place.

There is strength in staying the course, but there is divinity in joy.

She began to ask:

"What would this feel like if I allowed myself to enjoy it?"

"What if pleasure was not a distraction but a compass?"

She discovered that joy is not indulgence — it is information.

It tells you what aligns.

It tells you where your soul expands.

And when she let herself be guided by that expansion, even the challenging became holy.

So she transforms grind into grace and pressure into purpose.

Not by ignoring what is hard — but by bringing her full self to it.

With presence.

With intention.

With reverence.

The Queen does not endure life. She engages with it.

Responsibility, to her, is not heavy — It is the most sacred form of freedom.

Because when you stop avoiding your power, you realise:

You are not here to survive your life.

You are here to shape it and to enjoy it.

Chapter 26

The Queen Speaks: On Man, Power & Sacred Alignment

"Man is not the enemy. Misuse is. What we fight is distortion, not design.

We do not rise to conquer men — we rise to meet them as equals in evolution."

Let it be known — we are not here to invert the hierarchy, nor to mimic the structures that wounded us. We are here to transmute it all. To offer a new frequency.

There is a sacred masculine —

Strong like mountain.

Clear like river.

Present like firelight in winter.

He is not the patriarch who colonised the earth — He is the protector of the wild, the holder of space the mirror of truth.

The feminine does not wish to overthrow him.

She wants to awaken him.

To remember what he was before the world told him he had to dominate in order to be worthy.

And she must remember too — She is not small, nor secondary, nor a lesser version of his strength.

She is the seed of life, the keeper of cycles, the architect of intuition.

Together, they were always meant to dance.

Two flames. Two forces. Not the same, but symbiotic.

Not mirrored, but magnified by one another.

We must acknowledge our differences — not to divide — but to unlock the full spectrum of human potential.

Masculine presence. Feminine wisdom.

Direction and depth.

Protection and creation.

Together — not identical — but indispensable.

So we release the myth that man is the enemy.

We name the true enemy: fear.

Fear of surrender. Fear of softness. Fear of being.

Fear of the feminine's power. Fear of the masculine's healing.

We are not here to shame each other — We are here to reclaim each other.

Let our daughters rise without shrinking.

Let our sons grow without armouring.

Let our children learn from us what wholeness looks like — Not domination, not submission but dynamic alignment.

This is the Queen's decree:

Let the new world be built not by force, but by frequency.

Not by conquest, but by communion.

The feminine and the masculine — Not in opposition — But in sacred co-creation.

Chapter 27

Miracles

"Often when a woman reclaims her power, they call her dangerous. When the Earth reclaims hers, they call it unnatural."

What is a miracle?

It is not magic.

It is not mythology.

It is alignment so pure, so natural, it appears impossible in a world built on distortion.

We were taught that miracles must be male-authored, institution-approved, heaven-sent.

But miracles are Earthborn.

They are womb-born.

They rise from silence and soil and the spaces between control.

"The age of miracles is not gone — it is simply no longer societally-sanctioned."

Miracles were never owned by saints or sanctioned by scripture.

They were whispered in caves, howled into wind, birthed in blood and danced into being.

They were burned out of us — or so they thought.

But the Earth remembers. And so do we.

We are not waiting for miracles.

We are building them.

One seed, one rhythm, one radical act of sovereignty at a time.

"Build in silence. Let the sacred speak."

No press release.

No announcement.

Just presence.

Just pulse.

Just precision.

The new world will not arrive through policy.

It will arrive through pattern.

And the miracle is not someday — it is now.

It is you, awake in your body, aligned with your truth, refusing to shrink.

The Queen doesn't perform miracles.

She becomes one.

The Queen's Undeniable Insight

She leans in, not to whisper — but to invite.

Not to command — but to remind.

"You were never broken."

That is the deepest lie they fed you — that your worth had to be earned, your voice had to be softened, your power had to be apologised for.

But here, in the stillness beneath the noise, you remember:

You are not a role to be played.

You are a force to be reclaimed.

The Queen does not come to give you power.

She comes to show you where you left it.

Chapter 28

Sacred Contribution

Sacred Contribution in a Forgetful World - They taught us that service was submission.

That to serve was to shrink, to disappear, to bend ourselves into usefulness.

But that is not our way.

Service is not sacrifice.

It is sacred contribution.

To serve, in the Queen's world, is not to diminish — it is to devote.

Not to pour endlessly from an empty cup, but to offer what overflows from alignment.

True service is a fire in the bones — not for applause or performance, but because something within us aches to contribute. We have mentioned this before, yet it is important and we need to be reminded.

"If you cannot love people, serve the land."

"If you do not trust the world, tend the roots beneath it."

Gaia, too, remembers.

She has been ravaged — ridiculed, silenced, scorched, sold.

And still, she opens. Still, she breathes. Still, she receives.

In the quiet beneath the noise, there is a pulse — the rhythm of a world remembering herself through our hands, our art, our offerings.

This is the new service:

Not martyrdom, but meaning.

Not obedience, but offering.

Not guilt, but grace.

When the Queen remembers who she is, her hands ache to create something that lives beyond herself — not as legacy, but as healing.

She does not serve from guilt.

She serves from grounding.

She does not give herself away.

She gives herself to something worthy.

This is sacred reciprocity:

To give where we are received.

To plant what we were born to grow.

To offer not from depletion, but from remembrance.

And in this way, service becomes ceremony.

The soul's devotion made visible.

A prayer in motion.

The Deepest Understanding

"Every woman carries a sovereign flame.

When she tends to it with devotion, she doesn't need permission to shine. She simply radiates."

The Queen's deepest truth is not a fixed philosophy.

It is a living current, a stream of evolving wisdom that is nourished every time a woman remembers who she truly is.

She wants you to know:

You are not here to become someone else.

You are here to return.

Return to your rhythm.

Return to your knowing.

Return to your sacred yes and your powerful no.

Return to your sensual, untamed, divinely orchestrated self.

And from that place, you do not ask the world to change — you become the change the world never saw coming.

The Queen Evolves

The Queen is not a destination.

She is a constellation — alive, shifting, expanding with each woman who claims her wholeness.

There is no final word.

No neat ending.

Because you are the continuation.

You are the breath that keeps this alive.

A Call to Action

"Do not dim yourself to fit their comfort. Rise into your full frequency."

Write your truth.

Speak it aloud.

Live it in your choices.

Feel it in your body.

Let it ripple through your lineage.

Gather your sisters.

Cultivate your craft.

Reject the boxes.

Redefine beauty.

Protect your energy.

Expand your presence.

Refuse the conformity.

Refuse the shame.

Refuse the slow death of waiting for permission.

You are not here to play small in a world that needs your light.

You are not here to survive.

You are here to reign.

In grace.

In love.

In truth.

In flame.

Affirmations of the Queen

1. I release the need to shrink to be accepted — I expand to be remembered.

2. My presence is a force of nature. I move with grace, depth and purpose.

3. I release inherited fear and rise in my own rhythm of truth.

4. My body is sacred ground; I nourish it, honour it and listen to its wisdom.

5. I no longer seek permission — I claim space because I was born to.

6. I am a living expression of the divine feminine — untamed, grounded and free.

7. I choose power over people-pleasing, alignment over approval, and truth over silence.

8. Every time I honour my intuition, I strengthen my inner throne.

9. I am not here to fit into the world. I am here to help reimagine it.

10. I remember who I am — and I rise for every woman who forgot.

Chapter 29

We must remember

"Man is not the enemy. Misalignment is."

The Queen speaks not in division but in remembrance. She reminds us that the wound is not male. The wound is disconnection — from nature, from intuition, from self and from each other.

Masculine energy is not the destroyer. It becomes destructive only when stripped of consciousness and forced to dominate what it was meant to protect.

We are not here to overthrow the masculine.

We are here to realign with it. To bring the sacred back into its structure. To meet strength with clarity. To dance the ancient dance of polarities — in harmony, not hierarchy.

Let us acknowledge our differences. Let us celebrate the way we move differently through time, space, emotion and vision.

And let us not fear those differences, but use them effectively — as instruments in a greater orchestra of creation.

The Queen knows:

That love is not submission.

That power is not control.

And that unity does not mean sameness.

We were never meant to be in conflict with each other.

We were meant to remember each other.

And as she considers her musings a few particular ones jumped out:

"If the girls are broken, so is the world — and therein lies our sacred opportunity."

The Queen looks upon the world not with bitterness, but with eyes wide open. Culture is not just sick — it is dismembered. Pulled apart by systems that separated head from heart, soul from soil, body from belonging. A culture that praises performance but ignores presence. That worships speed but abandons stillness. That trains girls to please and boys to dominate — while shaming them both for feeling.

"This world was not built for wholeness. But we are here to remember how to rebuild."

She sees a planet where nature is burned for profit, love is traded for power and truth is manipulated into performance. But she does not collapse in despair. She holds the grief in one hand — and possibility in the other.

What if the collapse we fear is actually the clearing?

What if the broken systems are not failures, but false gods losing their grip?

What if the chaos is the necessary cracking open?

The Queen does not speak of war — she speaks of restoration.

Of a feminine intelligence that sees through the noise.

Of masculine energy not as the enemy but as the partner — to be realigned, not erased.

Of a society that has trained people to be useful but not sacred — and how that must end.

"We will not destroy the world to save it. We will love it back into coherence."

And so, she speaks of new blueprints. Culture as ceremony. Education as initiation. Economics as ecology. Leadership as stewardship. Love as liberation.

"The world isn't just broken — it's becoming.

Let us meet it with reverence and with fire."

The Beginning...

It is time...

Chapter 30

Why?

You may be surprised that this book was not created for an audience; instead it was a reminder of what I already knew. I just needed the vessel in which to compile the thoughts and the haunting wisdom of the Queen.

Admittedly I was not going to write another book… I felt it was pointless due to the vast abundance of books hitting the digital realm, but this one would not let me go.

The original trigger took place when I was researching Quantum Cryptography - to figure out what was needed in terms of cyber security and in that space I recognised that Quantum carries all possibility when it is invisible…

Something about that became the catalyst... I realised that invisibility held power. That was when the book The Invisibility Game started to take form. As I wrote that book, another one I did not intend to write, The Queen, started to emerge within the story. The women in the book kept referencing it - the excepts. As I continued to write - The Queen gained power and I recognised that I no longer was writing for an audience - instead I was being reminded what my soul already knew. Admittedly I thought I might keep it to myself as a project to reflect on... But no... She is ready to find her kin and to ignite them too. So I hope this ignites you and reminds you. Please let others know about her/the book. If you fancy reviewing it, then please do so... I know it is not perfect and that is the point...

I the meantime I am sending you love through the field...

Printed in Great Britain
by Amazon

6448a2f5-ede9-4e56-977d-6a29afabdf3fR01